Harold White

TOG

The Thomas Tallis Observer Greenwich

Ernst Klett Verlag
Stuttgart · Leipzig

TOG

Autumn term

What's in this number?

Hello everybody,

Welcome to our brand new school magazine. Sorry it took such a long time to write this, but we are really happy with the result now. We hope you'll like our magazine, too!
We would like to write about all the things happening here at Thomas Tallis – one magazine for every term of the school year. Our magazine is full of projects, interviews, quizzes and jokes – and you can find out a lot about Greenwich, too.
If you'd like to join our team, you can find us in the library on Thursdays at 2 o'clock.
Now, have fun reading about TTS and all the crazy things going on here … and look out for our next edition[1].
By the way, just a short note about our name: Thanks everyone for sending us mails and texts with some very interesting names. We decided to call it 'TOG', because for us it's short for 'together' … we're making this magazine together, and the Observer bit makes it sound really grown-up[2] and serious and full of quality.

[1]**edition** [ɪˈdɪʃən] Ausgabe • [2]**grown-up** [ˌɡrəʊn ˈʌp] erwachsen

But look at some of the other names people sent in – not bad, either:

Hi all, how about calling the new school magazine TOM TOM? Just to clear up what it means: The tom-tom is a drum. It comes from Native American or Asian cultures and it is a traditional means of communication. That's where the navigation system in your car got its name from.

WHAT ABOUT … tallis times or the blue people?

What about 'Symphony' because Thomas Tallis was a composer?

I think a new school magazine would be great and I would like 2 call it 'Tallis News'.

tallis telegraph, or tallis talk … hope you like my ideas ☺

OK, here is my idea: "Buzz". I'm pretty sure you can think of better names than that, so I look forward to reading them all here.

Hi ya, TALLIS L8TEST would be nice.

It has got to be +++Talisman+++, something charmed with power.

You should call it 'Tallis Talk'!

Thanks for all your suggestions. If you have a story, pictures or want to contact us feel free to e-mail us at: newsroom@tt.greenwich.sch.uk

Your newsroom team:

Tara, Sam and Daisy

Find three more names for the new magazine. Compare your ideas with those of a partner. Discuss them and choose the one you like best. Tell your class.

An interview with a new student

by Lisa Taylor, Year 8

Hi everybody,
Here's an interview that I did with a new student in our year, Rob. He's from Scotland. Find out more about him.

WHERE ARE YOU FROM?
I'm from Inverness. That's in Scotland, in the Highlands. It's in the East of Scotland. And about 50,000 people live there.

HOW OLD ARE YOU?
I'm 12 now, but when your magazine comes out I'll be 13.

WHY? WHEN IS YOUR BIRTHDAY?
My birthday is in October. It's on October 2nd.

WHAT IS YOUR ADDRESS?
In Inverness or in Greenwich? Well, my Inverness address was 15 High Street and now I'm here in Greenwich and we live in Greenwich High Road. Isn't that funny?

WHAT ARE YOUR HOBBIES?
My hobbies are football and basketball: I like sports a lot! And drama – I like drama and school plays. Of course I also have hobbies outside school – I love comics, and watching football. And I'm really into sudoku.

AND WHAT'S YOUR FAVOURITE COLOUR?
Green is a good colour. I hate pink.

“Is there anything you don't like in the school canteen?
– Yes, most of the food!”

WHAT IS THE NAME OF YOUR FAVOURITE BAND?
The Koolkats!

WHAT'S SO COOL ABOUT THEM?
Just listen to them and you'll know!

WHAT DO YOU LIKE AT SCHOOL?
At my old school, I liked Drama and Sport. And our German teacher was very nice. Here at TTS … well, PE lessons are cool. And I like your caretaker! He's very friendly and helpful.

HAVE YOU GOT ANY BROTHERS OR SISTERS?
Yeah, one sister. She's 14 and … no, I can't say that … I'm sure she'll read this interview.

HAVE YOU GOT ANY PETS?
Harry, he's my mouse. He's two, and he's white with one black ear.

WHAT DO YOU THINK IS DIFFERENT HERE AT TTS?
I don't really know, but after three weeks I think TTS is a really cool school. I like the blue school uniform, and the food is quite nice, too. But I must find a new football club – the Caley Jags in Inverness are just too far away!

Rob, thank you very much for this interview!

What other questions would you like to ask Rob? Write them down and make up the answers.
Why not act out the interview or interview a (new) student at your school?

A trip to Mudchute Farm

by Lisa Taylor, Year 8

At the end of last year, we all went on a trip to Mudchute Farm in Pier Street. Before we went, our teacher, Mrs Carter, showed us a brochure and told us that from the farm you can see Canary Wharf. And they've got lots of farm animals.

> **Did you know?**
>
> Mudchute Farm is one of Europe's largest city farms.

We wanted to be farmhands for the day, so we went there, got some information from Denise (she's the schools officer at the farm) about the animals, and then we helped at the farm.
The trip to the farm was funny, too, because it's not very far from our school. We went on the DLR to Mudchute Station, then we just followed the signs and walked past the stables into the main courtyard[1].

> **Did you know?**
>
> From London you can also take the D3 or D6 bus from Canary Wharf and get off at the Pier Tavern.

Denise was very nice. She told us that we mustn't shout because the animals get so nervous. We were nervous, too, and my friends had so many questions. I think we all wanted to do all the jobs at the same time.
I really really liked the pig shed, and it was nice to muck them out[2] because I like dirty jobs. But the best thing was to see the little pigs. When we got there, it was time for their milk. There were little bottles and we could feed them. We had a really great day at the farm. Of course, it's open all the year round, and you can go there with your family, too. You can even have your birthday party at the farm … Once I went in August because there was a guided bat walk[3]. Kenneth Greenway was our guide and showed us the bats – and we really found them with the farm's amazing bat-finding equipment[4]. There is a nice café but you can also bring your own sandwiches. I think it's great to have a farm in the centre of the city. And I definitely want to go there in April, when you can see the lambs at Mudchute – I love lambs, they are so cute, fluffy[5] and so lovable. Do you know what Farmer Tom told us? "We have a few llamas, too, to give things an international flavour!"

Here are two pictures of animals that I took. What do you think?

> *What about a trip you went on?*
> *Can you write an article about it, too?*
>
> *Have you got any nice animal photos you could send in to a competition? Have a competition in class. Describe your pictures and find the best snapshot.*

"Did you know your school trip?
– Yes. We're going again tomorrow.
Why?
– As a search party."

"A party of schoolchildren from the city went on a trip to the country. One of them found a pile[6] of empty milk bottles and shouted, 'Look, miss, I've found a cow's nest!'"

[1]**main courtyard** [ˌmeɪn ˈkɔːt jɑːd] Haupthof • [2]**to muck out** [mʌk ˈaʊt] ausmisten • [3]**guided bat walk** [ˈgaɪdɪd ˈbæt ˈwɔːk] Fledermaus-(beobachtungs)führung • [4]**equipment** [ɪˈkwipmənt] Ausrüstung • [5]**fluffy** [ˈflʌfi] flauschig, kuschelig • [6]**pile** [paɪl] Haufen

SAM'S PAGE

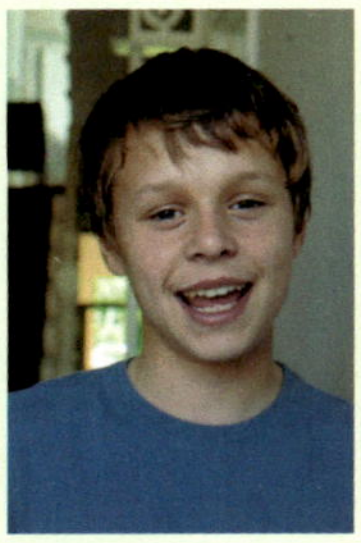

Hi,

My name is Sam Spencer. I live in Wendover Road in Greenwich. I'm in Year 8. My friends always make fun of me because they say I'm always late for everything, so I thought, 'Why not write a page for our new school magazine on excuses[1] and jokes?' What do you say when you're late for school? And what about homework?

Maybe you can also write to me and tell me about the funny things people in your year say when they're late or when they haven't got their homework? I can write about this in our next magazine.

Bye,
Sam

Here are some of my own favourites:

Teacher: You've been ten minutes late for school every day this year and all you do is come up with stupid excuses.

Pupil: I know. If I could be 15 minutes late, that would give me enough time to come up with better excuses.

Teacher: Do you have a good excuse for being late yesterday?

Pupil: If I had a good excuse for being late, I'd save it and use it for tomorrow.

We have a kid in our school who has never been on time for anything. He was two years old when he was born.

This is what you can say when you haven't got your homework:

I used it to fill a hole in my shoe; you wouldn't want it now.

I'm sorry I don't have my homework, but my friend hasn't finished copying it yet.

I didn't do it, because I didn't want the other kids in the class to look bad.

I lost it in a fight. There was this kid who said you weren't the best teacher in the school.

I gave it to a friend, but he suddenly moved away and now I haven't got it.

I left it in my shirt and my mother put it in the washing machine.

I'm sorry, sir, I put it in a safe, but lost the combination.

I haven't got my homework – my pet gerbils[2] had babies, and they used it to make a nest.

"**Mr Briggs:** Joseph, you've been late for school every day this week.
Joseph: No, Mr Briggs, I was only late for school four days this week. The other day I was absent."

What are your favourite excuses? Write them down.

[1]**excuse** [iks'kjuːs] Ausrede • [2]**gerbil** ['dʒɜːbɪl] Wüstenspringmaus

☼ **photos** ☼ **photos** ☼ **photos** ☼ **photos** ☼

We're going to have a photo competition in every TOG. You can win a card for your camera and a big poster of your photo. Do you want to have a look at all the photos from the competition? Then go to Room 20.

The title of January's competition is:

GREENWICH AS I SEE IT.

"**TEACHER:** Now, if I gave you three rabbits, then the next day I gave you five rabbits, how many would you have?
PUPIL: Nine, sir.
TEACHER: Nine?
PUPIL: Yes, sir. I've got one already!"

Foxes

by Bob Greenfell, Year 9

A boy in our class is really interested in wild animals. The other day, there was a fox in a dark hole under some planks near the garages of his house in Wendover Road. That got me interested in foxes, too. I spoke to Bruce Lindsay-Smith, a London fox hunter, and here is what I found out.

Mr Lindsay-Smith is a qualified fox 'wildlife manager'. He has been hunting urban foxes for more than 25 years. Sometimes, he shoots and traps[1] up to 10 foxes per night in the London area. "In many ways foxes are a victim of their own success[2]," he says. "From what I can see, there are more foxes in London than ever before."

And he is right – the red fox has become a familiar[3] sight in the city since arriving from the English countryside. Traditionally, English hunters used to chase[4] foxes with packs of hounds. Some people think there are now over 10,000 foxes in the capital. In Greenwich, some people have given up trying to control them. City councils[5] distribute leaflets informing householders that foxes are wildlife and we should learn to live in 'harmony' with them.

Mr Lindsay-Smith has many clients[6]: football clubs, garden designers, building companies, but also people with nice gardens. They don't like ruined lawns and excrement on the back patio. People also hate fleas or the foxes' mating cries[7] in the night.

Mr Lindsay-Smith says it's important to avoid cruelty when catching a fox. In some cases (because of campaigns by animal rights campaigners[8]) clients ask him to let the foxes go free in another part of London.

But some people think it's not a good idea to trap foxes and move them to another place, because other foxes will take their place. "All you're doing is creating a vacuum for another fox to fill." Usually, after he has caught a fox he shoots it with a pistol. "One shot is usually all I need. The fox is dead before it even hits the ground," he says.

So what can you do? Here are some tips:

- keep all rubbish bins tidy
- take away all food
- spray your gardens with chemicals
- make sure that fences have no gaps
- block off foxholes

[1]**to trap** [træp] einfangen • [2]**success** [sək'ses] Erfolg • [3]**familiar** [fə'mɪliə] vertraut • [4]**to chase** [tʃeɪs] jagen • [5]**city council** ['sɪtɪ 'kaʊnsl] Stadtrat, Stadtverwaltung • [6]**client** ['klaɪənt] Kunde, Kundin • [7]**mating cry** ['meɪtɪŋ ˌkraɪ] Paarungsruf • [8]**animal rights campaigner** [ˌænɪml 'raɪts kæm'peɪnə] Tierrechtler/-in

Foxes in cities are different. They don't run away from humans, they even curl up on the lawn like a cat. If people bang on the window they just slink away[9].

Nowadays, there is another problem – we are running out of places to put foxes, because they couldn't survive[10] in the country.

Foxes are most active from dusk to dawn[11]. During the December – January mating season, dog foxes will howl to scare rivals away from their territory. Cubs[12] usually appear in late March and April. Foxes born in towns rarely move to the country. They will kill chickens, rabbits and guinea pigs, but it is rare for them to attack cats.

Foxes have even made it into the Houses of Parliament, where one was found asleep on a cupboard. Another broke into the grounds of Buckingham Palace, killing some of Queen Elizabeth II's pink flamingos.

A survey in 2001 found that 80 percent of Londoners liked having the animals around. Some even attract foxes by putting out food for them to eat. This is not a healthy diet for the animals. Urban foxes usually only live for about 15 months.

I think foxes are really really interesting animals. And they are extremely clever, too. If you have a favourite animal, you can also write a short piece for our new school magazine.

What about your favourite animal? Can you put together a page about it? Maybe you can work with a partner.

[9]**to slink away** [ˈslɪŋkə ˈweɪ] wegschleichen • [10]**to survive** [səˈvaɪv] überleben • [11]**from dusk to dawn** [frəm ˈdʌsk tə ˌdɔːn] in den Nachtstunden (von der Abenddämmerung bis Sonnenaufgang) • [12]**cub** [kʌb] Junge(s)

More animals

Can you guess what these animals on the left are? Ask your Biology teacher, or use the Internet. Just to get you started: I took the picture in the Rocky Mountains.

Cutty Sark news

I'm sure you've all heard about the terrible fire on one of Greenwich's most important tourist attractions – the *Cutty Sark*. At the time, the ship was undergoing restoration[1] work, and about fifty per cent of the ship had been taken away, including the figurehead[2], the masts and rigging[3], the coach house[4], and most of the planking[5], so it could have been a lot worse.

Well, this was back in May 2007, and it was not quite the end for this fascinating ship. Here's some great news: The *Cutty Sark* can now be fully restored. This is thanks to a £3.3m gift from Israeli shipping magnate[6], Sammy Ofer (he served in the Royal Navy during the Second World War). The donations[7] from the Heritage Lottery Fund to the *Cutty Sark* rebuilding appeal[8] are now up from £10m to £23m. This means that the work can be completed in time for the 2012 Olympics, when more tourists are expected to visit London and Greenwich.

You can still send your own donations to the Cutty Sark Trust at 2 Greenwich Church Street, Greenwich SE10 9BG. You want to find out more about the *Cutty Sark* and see that the fire wasn't too bad really? Then go to the official website, it's very interesting: http://www.cuttysark.org.uk/

Our school is close to the *Cutty Sark*, but even people living in Greenwich don't know a lot about this ship. The *Cutty Sark* is the most famous tea clipper in the world. She was first launched[9] in Scotland in 1869. The name comes from 'Tam O'Shanter'; a poem by Robert Burns, where Tam meets a group of witches. Most of the witches are ugly, but there is one, Nannie, who is young and beautiful. In the poem, we learn that she only wears a 'cutty sark', i.e. a short shirt. The ship's figurehead is a representation of this beautiful witch.

Did you know?

The fire apparently broke out around 4.45 am on 21 May 2007.

The *Cutty Sark*'s shape[10] and an enormous area of sail made her the fastest ship in the tea trade[11] with China. Later, from 1885 to 1895, she was used in the wool trade with Australia, bringing new wool from Sydney to London, setting new speed records year after year.

In 1895, she was sold to the Portuguese and her crews called her *Pequina Camisola* ('little shirt'). In 1920 she was sold again and became the *Maria do Amparo*. In 1922 a British captain, Wilfred Dowman, bought her from the Portuguese owners. Dowman died in 1938 and his widow presented her to the Thames Nautical Training College at Greenhithe on the Thames, where she was used as a training ship.

After the Second World War she was taken to Greenwich and placed in a specially constructed dry dock in 1954. After a lot of restoration work she was opened to the public in 1957. Since then more than thirteen million people have visited her. In 2007 the ship was being restored again when a fire broke out, but the *Cutty Sark* should be ready for the Olympic Games in 2012 and the thousands of visitors who will want to see this famous Greenwich attraction.

[1]**restoration** [restə'reɪʃən] Reparatur und Erhaltung • [2]**figurehead** ['fɪgəˌhed] Galionsfigur • [3]**rigging** ['rɪgɪŋ] Takelage • [4]**coach house** ['kəʊtʃ ˌhaʊs] auf Deck gebaute Kabine • [5]**planking** ['plæŋkɪŋ] Planken • [6]**shipping magnate** ['ʃɪpɪŋ ˌmægneɪt] Großreeder/-in • [7]**donation** [deʊ'neɪʃən] (Geld-)Spende • [8]**appeal** [ə'piːl] (Spenden-)Aufruf • [9]**to launch** [lɔːntʃ] vom Stapel lassen • [10]**shape** [ʃeɪp] Form • [11]**tea trade** ['tiː ˌtreɪd] Teehandel

Where to eat in Greenwich

We all go to the canteen for lunch, of course, but do you get hungry on the way home? Going swimming straight after school? Need something to eat on Saturday or Sunday?

Our reporters Manelli and Jacky have been out and about in Greenwich testing local take-away snack bars. It's a tough job, but somebody has to do it!

++++	Excellent
+++	Very good
++	OK
+	Not so good
–	Don't go there!

All Fish ✦✦✦
Fried fish, meat and veggie pies, sausages.
Drinks in cans.
Great chips, fresh and thick.

Greenwich Chip Shop –
Fish 'n' chips, sausages.
Chips: terrible, soggy and cold. Yuk!

The Pie Shop ✦✦
Pies and pasties with everything you can think of and more. Pizza pieces, too.
No chips.

Jamey's Burger Van ✦
Burgers and hot dogs. OK if you like fried onions with everything! No chips.

Have your say

Is there something you want to tell people about? Whether it's chewing gum sticking to your shoes in the playground or people talking too loudly in the canteen, tell us about your 'pet hate'.

When we asked people about this, many of you told us: "What we really hate is new school magazines that you like a lot, and then, suddenly, they're no longer there."

So start writing to us to make sure TOG has a long and happy life!

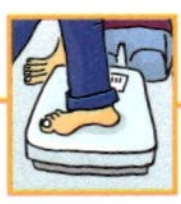

Question

How long does it take the average 10-year-old British kid to eat his or her own weight in chips?

6 months • 9 months • 1 year • 15 months • 18 months • 21 months • 2 years?

Answer: Between 9 months and 1 year, i.e. 35–40 kilos.

Lost and found

Under this heading, we're going to tell you about things that were found in our school. If you have lost something, you can also put it here, and maybe someone can help you?

Have you seen my tablets? They are really expensive and I left them in my anorak pocket in the gym. Maybe they fell out. I must take them every day. If you find them, don't eat them – they are dangerous for you!
Rob, Year 8

Found: a ticket for the London Eye. It was on my tray in the TTS Eatery on October 14th. If it is yours, please contact:
Tim Radman, Year 9

I can't find my new drumstick – I took it to school last Friday because I wanted to practise with the Tom-Toms. Please help me find it, it's important.
Terry

What about your messages? How can we help you?

QUIZ PAGE

SUDOKU

Sudoku rules are easy: Fill all empty squares so that the numbers 1–9 appear once in each row, column and 3x3 box. (The answers are on p. 32.)

		2	3		8			
9	3						7	1
7				4	1			
6	1	7			3			
	4	3				2	1	
			4			3	6	5
			5	8				3
4	9						5	6
			1		9	4		

PHOTO QUIZ !

Look at this detail from a picture taken at TTS. What is it? Write to us to win a prize.

FIND THE WORDS

All these words begin with 'F' and are in TOG stories and articles.

1.	F	O	X							
2.	F	I	S	H						
3.	F	O	U	N	D					
4.	F									
5.	F									
6.	F									
7.	F									
8.	F									

1. A wild animal in town and in the country. • 2. Good with chips. • 3. Not lost. • 4. Lambs are cute and … • 5. Llamas add an international … • 6. The caretaker at TTS is very … • 7. The Queen has these pink birds. • 8. The *Cutty Sark* has a witch as this.

There once was a
teacher from Leeds
Who swallowed a packet
of seeds.
In less than an hour …

Can you finish it?

Second best

Everybody knows the highest mountain in Britain is Ben Nevis (1,344 m or 4,409 feet), in Scotland. The second-highest mountain in Britain is in Scotland, too. But what's the name of it? And how high is it?

Ben Alder • Ben Lawers • Ben Macdui • Ben More

***Answer:** Ben Macdui at 1,309 m or 4,295 ft.*

TOG

Spring term

What's in this number?

Hello again,

We really managed to write another edition for this school year. After all your feedback, we've decided to make TOG a magazine for the younger students at our school – between 11 and 14. Older students already have their own *Thomas Tallis Magazine*.
So here's number 2 of TOG – that's very exciting. We got so many letters and e-mails from you that it was easy to fill all the pages.
And what can you read about this time? There's Sam's page again, with more jokes and excuses. You can find out about Greenwich and about the winner of our photo competition – GREENWICH AS I SEE IT. Also, our new section on stars tells you more about Shania Twain: There's plenty that you didn't know before. And would you like to write a piece for TOG?
So, enjoy the spring, and don't forget to go and watch the London Marathon in April … and don't eat too many of those Easter eggs.

Your newsroom team:

Tara, Sam and Daisy

SAM'S PAGE

Hi everybody,

Last time I wrote down some of my favourite jokes and excuses. Now so many of you have sent in your own jokes that there isn't enough space here to write them all down. Here are some of the best things sent to me, but you can still send more, and I'll put them in next time.

Bye,
Sam

And here are some excuses from people who didn't do their homework:

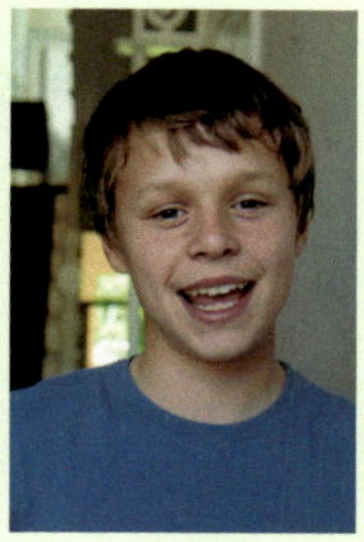

Another pupil fell in a lake, and I jumped in to rescue him. My homework drowned.

I was late because it was foggy this morning and I couldn't find my way to school.

My little sister ate it.

The best excuses:

TEACHER: Do you have any idea how many times you've been late for school this year?
PUPIL: Well, miss, I don't think it's been more than once a day.

TEACHER: Why are you late for school again?
PUPIL: I stopped two boys fighting, sir.
TEACHER: Well done. How did you manage that?
PUPIL: I kicked both of them, sir.

PUPIL: I'm sorry I'm late, sir. I was having a dream about football.
TEACHER: How did that make you late for school?
PUPIL: They played extra time.

TEACHER: Why didn't you come to school yesterday?
PUPIL: While I was walking to school, my shoes fell apart[1]. I went back home to see if I had any more. But my trainers were in the washing machine and my mum wouldn't let me leave the house without any shoes.

After I talked to some of my teachers, they wanted me to put in something about what teachers say, too — and what they really mean:

Karen has an endless energy. (The little monster can't sit still for five minutes.)

Your son really loves interaction with his peers[2]. (Your son needs to stop socialising[3] and start working.)

Your daughter is an adventurous nature lover who rarely misses opportunities to explore new territory. (She was caught skipping school[4] at the fishing pond.)

Some students hide their emotion, but X is very expressive and open. (X is always complaining[5].)

How many words do you know for 'missing school' – even if you don't do it?
'Play truant' is the official phrase, but people also 'skip school', 'bunk off', 'skive', 'dog it' (but only in Scotland!).

[1]**to fall apart** [ˌfɔːlə ˈpɑːt] auseinanderfallen • [2]**peer** [ˈpɪə] Gleichaltrige/-r • [3]**socialising** [ˈsəʊʃəlaɪzɪŋ] unter Leuten sein • [4]**to skip school** [ˈskɪp ˈskuːl] die Schule schwänzen • [5]**to complain** [kəmˈpleɪn] sich beklagen

photo competition · photo competition

Last time, we asked you to send in your photos for our competition. Thanks to everyone who liked our idea. We can tell you we had so many great photos it was hard to choose the ones to make it into the magazine: but here they are – Greenwich as you see it ... what do you think?

The winners of the "Greenwich as I see it" competition are:
Becky Miller, Year 8 – 3rd prize
Lisa Taylor, Year 8 – 2nd prize
Bob Brent, Year 9 – 1st prize

Bob

Yes, we all know this lady!

Lisa

Becky

Our final competition for this school year is on **"Sports Day"** – take lots of pictures, and don't forget to take a look at all the other Greenwich pictures in Room 20!

My favourite: Shania Twain

by Jennifer Redman, Year 8

My favourite star is Shania Twain. Did you know that her album *Come On Over* was the most successful female solo artist album of all time? It sold 34 million copies worldwide!

Her single "I'm Gonna Getcha Good!" shows a typical Shania attitude[1] in the lyrics: It's all about a girl who knows what she wants, she not only knows how to get it, but she's going to "get it good".
"Ka-Ching!" is one of my all-time favourite songs because Shania is so cheeky[2] on it. It's also critical of our modern life, how commercial and crazy about money society has become – people only want to go shopping; they shop, shop, shop and then shop some more.
I'm also fascinated by her because she is what people call a cross-over artist – she has won prizes for her country music but she's also a very sexy pop-singer.

Shania Twain was born in Canada on August 28, 1965. She is the second oldest of five children. She grew up with her stepfather, an Ojibway Indian named Jerry Twain, and her mother, Sharon. When she was a child her family was very poor. Sometimes they had no food, but there was always a lot of music in the house.
Shania learned to play the guitar and often played on her own in her bedroom. Her family listened to many different styles of music. Her mom noticed Shania's talents and soon took her to radio and TV studios, community centres, senior citizens' homes, "everywhere they could get me booked". In the summer, Shania worked with her stepfather in the Canadian bush, where she learned to use a chain saw[3] as well as any man. In the winter season, Shania often did television and radio performances.

When she was 21, Shania lost her parents in a car accident. She took on the role of mum to her three brothers and managed to keep the household going. When her brothers were grown enough to look after themselves, Shania gave up her real name, Eileen, and adopted the Ojibway name of Shania, meaning 'I'm on my way.'

Twain recorded a demo tape of original music and sent it to a record company. They liked her music and her first records were quite successful. In 1993 she made her second album, *The Woman in Me*, with the help of producer Robert John Lange, who is known as 'Mutt'. In December of that year Shania and Mutt married and when *The Woman in Me* came out in the spring of 1995 it sold 18 million copies. This made Shania the best-selling female country artist of all time. The single "Any Man of Mine" became the first of four No. 1 hits in a row[4] for Twain, including "If You're Not in It for Love", "I'm Outta Here!", "You Win My Love" and "No One Needs to Know". The album won a Grammy for country album of the year and was named album of the year 1995 by the Academy of Country Music.
Twain's third collection, *Come on Over*, was released in 1997. Two singles from this album became No. 1 hits: "Honey, I'm Home" and "Love Gets Me Every Time". Her ballad "You're Still the One" went to No. 1 on the country singles chart and made it to No. 2 on Billboard's Hot 100 pop chart.

[1]**attitude** ['ætɪtjuːd] Einstellung • [2]**cheeky** ['tʃiːkɪ] frech • [3]**chain saw** ['tʃeɪn ˌsɔː] Kettensäge • [4]**in a row** [ɪnə 'rəʊ] hintereinander

At the end of 1999, Shania and her husband moved to Switzerland. In the summer of 2001 they welcomed their first child together while preparing Shania's 2002 album *Up!*, featuring the hits "I'm Gonna Getcha Good" and "Forever and For Always".
In 2004, Shania's album *Greatest Hits* came out, which included a duet with Billy Currington, "Party For Two".

You can find out more about Shania Twain's life, if you want to. Go to her official website:
http://www.shaniatwain.com/news.asp

Do you have any more up-to-date information on Shania Twain?

What about your favourite star? Would you like to write a piece for TOG?

Swap shop

We were quite surprised to see how many people wrote to us about things they didn't want … and things they were looking for.

Now how does this section work? If you are interested in something in the "wanted" or "offered" sections, just talk to us, and we can put you in touch with the person looking for or offering help/items. (That's why we've put their initials after the ad – so we know who they are!)

Wanted:

Someone to eat my packed lunches – my mum always gives me too much to eat, and I don't want to throw the food away. (PB)

Video of the fire on the Cutty Sark (for a school project). (ST)

Ticket for the concert at the O2 on June 21. (It's a birthday present for my sister but the concert's sold out!) (OM)

Rollerblades, any size (Charity shop in Greenwich)

Help with the garden: My granny is looking for students who can cut the grass, water her flowers, etc. (LR)

Who can teach me to play chess? (KR)

Offered:

Stamp collection, Animals of Britain 2009 (ON)

Trainers size 9 (used one term). (JA)

Help with your computer for free! (MF)

Great books – I've never read them all but can't keep them in our house. (DN)

"Did you hear about the schoolboy who put on a clean pair of socks every day? By the end of the week he couldn't get his shoes on."

Have your say

In our first edition of TOG, we asked people to tell us about their 'pet hate'. A lot of people wrote or mailed us. But please don't forget your name and your tutor group – we cannot print your article without them. So here are two 'pet hates'.

What I really hate is how difficult it is for young people to find a place, outside school, to just sit and talk. If you go to a café the waitress always comes and asks you: "Anything else?" What she really means is: "When are you leaving?" It's not fair at all, because often there are lots of empty tables and it would be OK to just sit there. They know that kids haven't got much money.

Julia Clifton, Year 8

My pet hate is public transport. I really hate it when young people are together in a group and want to talk and have fun, but the other people on the train think we are too noisy. It's different on the underground, most people are very quiet down there and I can see that it's not nice when you have a group of noisy teenagers or tourists right next to you. But have you ever noticed that nobody tells grown-ups not to be noisy on a train? Sometimes they are terrible, but it is usually the teenagers that get told off.

Rob Zaphania, Year 7

School jokes puzzle

After all that hate, let's have a bit of fun: Here are four jokes about school – but they are all mixed up. Can you try and find out what goes where?

Titles:
Writing in the dark
A wise schoolteacher
Bottom of the class
The English teacher

Punch lines:
"It says that you need to write more clearly!"
"They still teach the same thing at both ends."
"Oh, I'll turn the light off and you can just sign this letter from school for me."
"I'll promise not to believe everything he or she says happens at home."

Main parts:
A wise schoolteacher sends this note to all parents on the first day of school: "If you promise not to believe everything your child says happens at school …"

An English teacher often wrote little notes on student essays. She was working late one night, and as the hours passed, her handwriting got worse and worse. The next day a student came to her after class with his essay she had corrected. "I can't make out what you wrote on my paper." The teacher took the paper, looked at it for a minute, and then said, …

"I'm worried about you always being at the bottom of your class," said the father to his son. "Don't worry, Dad," he replied. …

Little Johnny asked his father, "Dad, can you write in the dark?" His father said, "I think so. What do you want me to write?" Little Johnny replied, …

Recipes

You know how much we love cookery classes. Here are some simple recipes that you can all try – and if they don't work, you can eat at the TTS Eatery!

Cauliflower[1], date and banana salad

1 cauliflower
50 g dates[2] (take the stone out)
2 bananas
150 ml mayonnaise
lemon juice
salt and pepper

Break the cauliflower into small pieces; cook in or over boiling water for 5 minutes. Cool quickly. Chop the dates and the bananas. Mix the mayonnaise and lemon juice. Put everything in a salad bowl and mix well. Add a little salt and pepper.

Coconut biscuits

100 g butter/margarine
100 g flour (self-raising[3] or use baking powder)
100 g dark brown sugar
100 g desiccated[4] coconut
pinch of salt
1 egg

Turn the oven on at 180°. Rub the butter into the flour until it's like fine crumbs. Stir in the sugar, coconut and salt. Mix well, stir in the egg, mix to a soft dough. Roll out thinly and cut into rounds. Place on a baking sheet and bake at 180° for about 15 minutes until golden brown.
Makes 20 biscuits.

"Tom (sees broccoli on his plate): 'Hey, Mum, what's this? I can't eat trees, not even small ones!'"

Cream of leek soup

2 large leeks[5]
1 small potato
1 carrot
25 g butter/margarine
1.2 l vegetable stock[6]
salt, pepper
150 ml fresh cream

Chop the vegetables. Melt the butter and fry the vegetables on a low heat for a few minutes. Add the stock, salt and pepper, bring to a boil, simmer[7] for 20 minutes. Put the soup in the blender[8] for a few seconds, stir in the cream and enjoy.

Melting moments

100 g butter/margarine
75 g white or brown sugar
1 egg
125 g flour (self-raising or use baking powder)
1/4 teaspoon salt
cornflakes

Turn the oven on at 180°. Mix the butter and sugar, add the egg and mix well. Add the flour and salt and stir gently. When the dough is well-mixed, put a handful of cornflakes on a piece of kitchen paper, cover with another piece of paper and crush[9] the cornflakes into smaller pieces. Take a teaspoonful of dough and drop it onto the crushed cornflakes. Put some flour on your (clean!) hands and roll the dough until it is covered in cornflakes. Place them on a baking sheet. Continue until you have used all the dough. Bake them at 180° for about 15 minutes until golden.
Tip: If you are a chocolate fan, dip them into melted chocolate after baking.

[1]**cauliflower** ['kɒlɪflaʊə] Blumenkohl • [2]**date** [deɪt] Dattel • [3]**self-raising** [self 'reɪzɪŋ] Mehl, dem Backpulver beigemischt ist • [4]**desiccated** ['desɪkeɪtɪd] geraspelt • [5]**leek** [liːk] Lauch • [6]**stock** [stɒk] Brühe, Fond • [7]**to simmer** ['sɪmə] köcheln • [8]**blender** ['blendə] Mixer • [9]**to crush** [krʌʃ] zerdrücken

A Greenwich project (from 7CE)

Our class wanted to do a project about Greenwich. But then our teacher had a brilliant idea: We all went on a tour of Historic Greenwich with a real guide first – and we learnt so much. The tour started with a fantastic boat ride from the Tower of London. We passed Tower Bridge, went past the Docklands and after about three miles we reached Greenwich – what a fantastic sight: Maritime and Royal Greenwich! So we learnt lots of things about the sea and the Royal Navy, and lots about the kings and queens who have lived here. We really wanted to find out what a tourist would learn about our home town. There are people from all over the world who come here to look at the Royal Observatory, the Queen's House, the Royal Naval College, and even the Fan Museum. (No, it's not about football fans! If you want to find out more about beautiful ladies' fans, check out their homepage. Use your search engine and 'Greenwich Fan Museum'.)

After this official tour, we went back to school and thought about all this new information: What would young tourists really like to learn about Greenwich? How interesting is all this history to a 12-year-old from another country? Our class came up with an answer: Learning about the history of Greenwich is important, of course, and it is the key to Greenwich, the River Thames and the Prime Meridian. But kids our age want to learn about other things, so we came up with our own tour of Greenwich – a tour that has bits of history, but also tells kids what it's like to live here in Greenwich, where we go after school, what we do on Saturdays, how we spend our holidays here. And then Mr Keeper had another of his crazy ideas – he told us it would be nice to take a look at Greenwich under Greenwich … not just the bit that we know on top, but the other world down below: the scary foot tunnel, the emergency exits of the underground, etc. Next month, we'll try the tour on our exchange partners from France. They'll love it!

Can you do your own tour of places near where you live?

"JANE: Mum, I've been banned from cookery lessons because I burnt something.
MOTHER: Well, that doesn't sound too terrible. What did you burn?
JANE: The school kitchen."

What teachers say

Here is what some of the teachers and pupils at TTS said this school year:

SIMON: Sir, is there life after death?
MR BROWN: Why do you ask?
SIMON: I may need the extra time to finish all this homework you gave us.

MS THOMPSON: Your homework yesterday was to draw a map of Britain including all the rivers. Why didn't you finish it?
TINA: I ran out of paper. I thought you wanted it life size.

MR ERICSON: If this class doesn't stop making so much noise, I'll go crazy!
CLASS 8: Too late, sir, we haven't made a sound for an hour!

MR BLACK: Who broke the window?
JIM: It was him, sir. He ducked when I threw a stone at him.

What about your class?
What did your teachers say?

A GREENWICH QUIZ!

Oh, yes, you think you know Greenwich ... but even if you live here there's much more for you to find out.

Have a go at the following questions. Which of these statements is true?

1 The Romans did not live in Greenwich.

2 In August 1588, Elizabeth I travelled from Greenwich to Tilbury to look at her ships before their fight against the Spanish Armada.

3 The 'Tulip[1] Staircase' in the Queen's House with its spiral[2] stone steps was the first of its kind in England.

4 The Great Hall in the Queen's House is round.

5 The Royal Naval College had to be split in two because Queen Mary – who lived in the Queen's House – wanted to keep her view[3] of the river.

6 In 1884, at a conference in Washington, delegates from 25 nations decided that the world's prime meridian should be at Greenwich.

7 In the 19th century, 50 % of world commerce[4] used Greenwich to set their clocks by.

8 The last London dock closed in 1962.

9 In Greenwich, one of London's oldest buildings stares across the river at one of London's newest.

10 Greenwich is a World Heritage Site[5] like the Taj Mahal in India.

11 Canary Wharf handled produce that arrived from the Canary Islands.

12 During school holidays, there are free events at the National Maritime Museum.

The Pier Fish Restaurant: the best fish 'n' chips in town. Special prices for TT pupils!

***Answers:** 1, 2, 3 are true but 4 is false: The Great Hall is a perfect cube. 5 and 6 are true, 7 is not quite true, it was over 70%. 8 is also false, it was 1981. 9 is true: One of the oldest buildings is the Greenwich Observatory which is opposite Canary Wharf Tower on the other side of the river. And 10 is true, so are 11 and 12.*

[1]**tulip** ['tjuːlɪp] Tulpe • [2]**spiral** ['spaɪrəl] spiralförmig • [3]**view** [vjuː] Aussicht • [4]**commerce** ['kɒmɜːs] Geschäftswelt • [5]**World Heritage Site** [ˌwɜːld 'herɪtɪdʒ ˌsaɪt] Weltkulturerbe

QUIZ PAGE

PLACES IN GREENWICH

What are these Greenwich names? The numbers tell you how many letters there are in the other words that make up each name. There is one letter too many in each name. Collect these extra letters. (The answers are on p. 32.)

A A H I L L F S T S T O M (6, 6 School) ____________ ____________

S U T T K A R M C Y (5, 4) ____________ ____________

O R S O V B T A Y R E M (Royal 11) ____________________

P I M M I D E R E R I N A S (5, 8) ____________ ____________

Q E U E S H A 'S O U N E (6, 5) ____________ ____________

L E N A L U V O C E G A L (Royal 5, 7) ____________ ____________

A S H M E N T (River 6) ____________

Put the letters you have collected together with an E and U to make the name of

a visitor attraction in Greenwich. (3, 6) ____________ ____________

DEFINITIONS

Match the word with the correct meaning.

1. cauliflower → E
2. cornflakes
3. leek
4. play truant
5. trainers
6. single
7. tulip
8. commerce

A a long white and green vegetable
B stay away from school
C a spring flower
D a CD with one song
E a round white and green vegetable
F shoes for sport
G business and trade
H food for breakfast

A WORD SNAKE

Make a snake with the words from these definitions. The last letter of the first word is the first letter of the next word, and so on.

1. short bits of time 2. cold food 3. a sweet fruit 4. More time at the end of a game is ... time. 5. singer, poet, painter 6. Shania's family name

moments____

Now make up your own word snake game for your partner to play.

TOG

Summer term

What's in this number?

Hi again,

This is the third and last edition of TOG for this school year. We are so happy to have given our school a new magazine. Lots of people have written to us to say how they liked our stories and our reports.
This time, there's even more fun: You can find out about the London Marathon and try our London quiz. There is a fantastic story from a French student, and you'll learn why our school is famous in Germany. We finish with a puzzle page as usual; you can read about the Thames Barrier and we also have some tips on what to read this summer.
And if you're really bored in the holidays, why not write an article for us that we can publish in TOG No. 4 at the beginning of next school year?

Have a great summer!

Your newsroom team:

Tara, Sam, Terry and Daisy

"School is over. School is done. We can stop learning and start having fun."

How my mum ran the London Marathon

by Kirsty Shaw, Year 9

Every year, people run in the London Marathon, and we all stand there and cheer them on[1]. But have you ever thought about who these people are? And why they do it? Well, for me it was very different, because my mum decided to run the Marathon … my mum – oh my God, how embarrassing[2], I thought. She's forty and she's not very fit and …

Well, let me tell you what happened. My mum got to know about *Shelter*[3]. It's a charity that helps people who are homeless. We all know there are lots of homeless people in London, and Mum wanted to help. So she put her name on the list for their team, and this is what they offered:

- Training, health tips and a 16-week training programme.
- Tips on how to raise more money[4].
- A groovy *Shelter* running vest to wear on the day of the Marathon.
- A free *Shelter* T-shirt for each of her supporters, as a great souvenir of the day and to help you to find each other in the crowd.
- Massages, refreshments and hot showers after the Marathon.

Well, I still didn't understand how this could work, but my mum told me that she wanted to ask her friends for money for the charity. This means they sort of 'paid' her for running the Marathon. She talked to a lot of people and most of them said: "We'll give you one pound for every mile you run." Well, they thought that Mum would stop after two or three miles, but she didn't … no, I'm really proud of my mum now, because she finished the London Marathon in just 4 hours 39 minutes! That's something I couldn't do!

And she raised over £ 1,200 – money that helped people to stay in their flats or to find a new home.

More information about running for

Shelter

The Housing and Homeless Charity.

Find it online at:
http://england.shelter.org.uk/what_you_can_do/running

What does *Shelter* do?

Shelter helps people who are homeless or may become homeless. It runs advice centres and gives special help to children and young people and to very old people who are without a home.

Shelter also has another important role. It campaigns for better housing and more help for people who don't have much money. It tries to change the government's ideas on housing so that more people can have their own home.

Click on "about us" to find out more details about ***Shelter*** and what the charity does.

Is there anyone out there who knows about *Shelter* and who can tell us more about their work? We're looking forward to your letters!

[1]**to cheer someone on** [ˌtʃiə sʌmwʌn ˈɒn] jmdn. anfeuern • [2]**embarrassing** [ɪmˈbærəsɪŋ] peinlich • [3]**shelter** [ˈʃeltə] Schutz, *hier:* Name einer Wohltätigkeitsorganisation • [4]**to raise money** [ˌreɪz ˈmʌni] Geld aufbringen

A QUIZ ON LONDON!

Here are some questions about London that you can try and answer over the holidays, or whenever you visit London. Find the answers at the end – but don't cheat! :-)

> "What did I learn? I don't remember and I'm not gonna try till next September."

1 Which are London's top three free visit attractions?
- the British Museum
- the National Gallery
- the National Portrait Gallery
- the Natural History Museum
- the Science Museum
- Tate Modern
- the Victoria and Albert Museum

2 The City of London is also called
- the Square Metre.
- the Square.
- the Square Mile.
- the Square Yard.

3 What do you think is the oldest building in London?
- St. Paul's Cathedral
- the Millennium Dome
- the Tower of London
- the Houses of Parliament
- Buckingham Palace

4 London is the biggest city in the UK with a population of about 8 million. But which is the second-largest city in the UK?
- Birmingham
- Glasgow
- Manchester
- Edinburgh
- Cardiff
- Belfast

5 Which is the longest line on the London Underground?
- the Circle Line
- the Central Line
- the Jubilee Line
- the Northern Line

> "**Little Monster:** I hate teachers! **Mother Monster:** Well, just eat your salad up then, dear!"

TTS London Walking Talks

Come and join one of our fine Walking Talks with our own TTS guides.
To go on a Walking Talk in London, meet your guide and other walkers on the pavement just outside the Underground station. You don't have to book. A Walking Talk doesn't cost any money – but all contributions to charity (e.g. *Shelter*) are gratefully received. The tours take about one-and-a-half hours. We offer a Greenwich under Greenwich tour, but you can also go on a Beatles tour, a Docklands tour from Canary Wharf or a tour about Shakespeare.
We do the tours on Wednesdays after school in the summer and on the first and third Saturday of every month, starting at 10.30 am. There's a list on the noticeboard and on the TTS website.
To find out more about our Walking Talks, contact Shana, Daisy, George or Harry in 8SG.

***Answers:** 1. The three most popular visitor attractions in London are the British Museum, the National Gallery and the Natural History Museum. 2. The City of London is also called the 'Square Mile'. 3. The Tower is London's oldest building. 4. The second biggest city in the UK is Birmingham. 5. The Central Line is the longest line on the London Underground.*

Fabien Chapuis

Hi everybody,
I'm a French student from Toulouse. I love England, and I have many friends here. Last time I stayed with a family in Manchester, but this time I'm doing a language course at the GSE, that's the Greenwich School of English. Maybe you people at TTS don't realize, but hundreds of students from all over the world come to Greenwich to learn English here. Most of us live with host families – my host family are the Jacksons, and their son Terry has asked me to write this page for your school magazine.
At the GSE, we play a lot of games, we sing songs and we do role plays – in English, of course. There are also lots of sports activities to choose from. Besides, I enjoy going into London to have a look at some of the sights or to go shopping. My friends in France are really jealous, I can tell you … and my sister wants to come and get to know Terry, because I sent her a photo and she liked him a lot.
At the school, we also have to write stories, and our teachers correct them. Terry likes my stories, especially when he is in them. For your magazine, I've written a story about a scary dream. How do you like this? And do you think you can write about your own dreams or nightmares, too? Why not send them to Terry, and maybe next time you can read your story in this magazine.
I'm going back to France in two weeks' time. Have you ever been to France? It's not very far for you at all, you just hop on the train and get from London to Paris. Maybe you can come and see me in Toulouse one day.

Yours, Fabien

A nightmare

by Fabien Chapuis

One evening, I was lying in bed and my dad was reading a story to me. I didn't like the story and when I fell asleep I had a terrible nightmare. In my dream, I was a fly. Together with my friends we spent all day flying around our world. Of course, we didn't know that our world was a small room, and we couldn't leave this room. And then the monster came: He wasn't really a monster, but to a fly he looked very, very big. My friends and I were sitting on this sandwich – it was his sandwich – and the monster took a newspaper and tried to kill us. I was fast enough to fly away, but seven of my friends died. The monster was very happy. "Seven, seven of them!" he shouted, and he was laughing. I was shocked. And then I wasn't a fly, but I was a little bird, and the monster put me in his pocket and left the room. I felt so happy because I thought now I could see the world and fly around. But the monster put his hairy hand into his pocket and I couldn't get out. "Mmh," he said. "I can eat this for lunch later." He walked around for a bit and then he got into a fight with another monster. They wanted to see who was stronger, and 'my' monster said, "OK, let's throw stones and see who can throw them higher." The other monster laughed and threw a stone … and it went high into the air … and came back after a very long time. But then the hairy hand got me out of the pocket and threw me, and of course I flew away and did not fall back down, so 'my' monster won. Oh, it was so nice to fly around, but suddenly I wasn't a bird, I was a real stone, and I started falling down, down, down … and when I woke up, I was lying on the floor in my room, and a fly was sitting on my nose.

TTS goes to Germany

You probably won't believe this, but did you know that our school is famous in Germany? Why?

Well, in Germany everybody has to learn English at school. Students usually start in primary school, and when they go on to another school at the age of ten they get their first real course book. In these course books, German students learn about a number of families and about one town or city in Britain. And believe it or not, there is a course book set in Greenwich! Our school is in it, with some of our students, the teachers, our caretaker and even our cafeteria. Of course, there is a lot about the Docklands, about Greenwich Park, even about Greenwich foot tunnel and the *Cutty Sark*. Now that's scary, isn't it?

Here's one page from the book, so you won't think I'm a liar[1]:

Want to find out more? You can have a look at the books, just go to: http://www.klett.de

"Why don't elephants ride bicycles? They haven't got thumbs to ring the bell with!"

photo competition photo competition

And the winner is ...

Yes, here we go again. We're getting more and more fantastic photos – make sure you have a look at them in Room 20.

Philip Wellmann, Year 8 – on his bike

Sports Day

"The teacher told one of the bad dressers in our class to do something about his shirt tail hanging out. So the boy took off his trousers!"

[1]**liar** [ˈlaɪər] Lügner/-in

SAM'S PAGE

Hi,

For this last edition of our magazine, I've chosen some of the best jokes and excuses again.

So many people have told me they really like my page … even the teachers are waiting for a good excuse now every time I'm late. But I try to be on time for my lessons.

Anyway, I'm looking forward to more jokes, and we can include them after the summer holidays. Have a great summer, see you all in Year 9,

Sam

A good excuse when you are late:

TEACHER: You're late again!
PUPIL: Sorry, sir, I overslept.
TEACHER: You mean you sleep at home as well as here?

TEACHER: Why are you late?
PUPIL: I must have over-washed, sir.

TEACHER: Why are you late?
PUPIL: Sorry, sir, the sign outside the school says, 'GO SLOW, CHILDREN!'

One day I was late to class and the teacher asked why. I simply told him that I was late because the bell rang before I got there. It got me out of a detention[1] so I was happy.

And why did people not have their homework?

I really wanted to get my homework done, but my mother said I need to get more rest at night.

A man came to me and said, "Your homework or your life!" I couldn't possibly give him my life so I gave him my homework.

[1]**detention** [dɪ'tentʃən] Nachsitzen

Here's a nice joke for the summer:

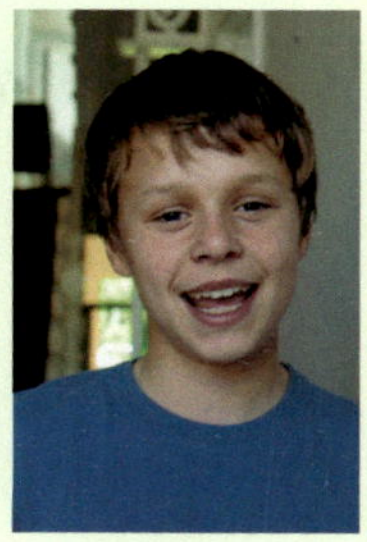

TEACHER: Well, class, this year's outing will be to the seaside.
CLASS: Hooray!
TEACHER: It will cost fifty pounds …
CLASS: Boo!
TEACHER: … by train, or two pounds by coach.
CLASS: Hooray!
TEACHER: The headmaster will be coming …
CLASS: Boo!
TEACHER: … to see us off.
CLASS: Hooray!
TEACHER: The weather will be wet and windy …
CLASS: Boo!
TEACHER: … in China and warm and sunny in England.
CLASS: Hooray!
TEACHER: There will be no paddling …
CLASS: Boo!
TEACHER: … until we get there.
CLASS: Hooray!
TEACHER: Lunch will be boiled fish and cabbage …
CLASS: Boo!
TEACHER: … for me and crisps, Coke and chocolate for you.
CLASS: Hooray!
TEACHER: There will be a visit to the museum …
CLASS: Boo!
TEACHER: … or, if preferred, to the funfair.
CLASS: Hooray!
TEACHER: But we must be back by twelve o'clock …
CLASS: Boo!
TEACHER: … midnight!
CLASS: Hooray!

Where to eat in Greenwich

Hi, they're back again – our reporters Manelli and Jacky have been out and about in Greenwich one more time, testing more local take-away and snack bars. This time, they had a look at food from different parts of the world. Again, a tough job, but somebody has to do it.

++++	Excellent
+++	Very good
++	OK
+	Not so good
–	Don't go there!

The Curry Prince ✦✦✦✦

Chicken Tikka Massala – in 5 minutes. Just 5 meals on the menu. Great prices. Cleanest place in town. No chips.

Chopsticks ✦✦✦

Asian fast food – really fast!
Hot and cold drinks.
Good value[1], rice and noodles, no chips.

The Hot Potato ✦✦

Baked potatoes with a great choice of salads and vegetables. Usually fast, but you may have to wait 15–20 minutes for your potato. Drinks in cans only.

Have your say

You know what really makes me angry? When people talk about their plans for the holidays from April through till July. I think people our age know that not everybody is rich and can afford[2] to travel to far-away places. Sometimes when I listen to people in the TTS Eatery I think it's like a competition … who can come up with the most expensive holiday, who spends most hours on the plane. It's very hard to say something like: "Oh, we don't have any money for a holiday this year, so I'm staying at home with a few good books. And I'm planning to go for a walk with my granny every day." Why not? Actually, I think we should all try and be a bit more sensitive[3] about this.

Julian Gray, Year 9

Any more out there? We'd like to have them ready for our autumn edition of TOG … Year 2, wow!

Swap shop

Our swap shop has become a great success – and people have stopped throwing away old things. So here are some more:

Wanted:

Sudoku puzzles: I'm addicted to them and I can never get enough … maybe you've got a collection at home that you don't want?

Old picture postcards of Greenwich. We're putting together an album for my grandparents' golden wedding: What did Greenwich look like in the 1950s and 60s?

Harry Potter 5: Yes, I've read 1–4, but 5 isn't in Greenwich library, and I haven't got the money to buy it. Can anyone lend it to me?

Offered:

I can look after your dog or cat when you're away on holiday. Very moderate prices.

Vacancy – one room in our holiday cottage in France. 4–19 August. Who would like to join us? Girls only!

[1]**value** ['vælju:] Wert • [2]**to afford** [ə'fɔ:d] sich leisten • [3]**sensitive** ['sentsɪtɪv] verständnisvoll, empfindsam

A visit to the Thames Barrier

by Andy Robbins, Year 7

This year, our class visited the Thames Barrier and the Information and Learning Centre. At first we all thought this is just something tourists do, but that's not true. When I first looked at the Thames Barrier I thought: So? What's so special about this? Why do people think it's the eighth wonder of the world?
Then we went to the centre: small, but very interesting – I like the idea that you have to walk through the cafeteria and ask the lady to open the door for you! :-). The man who gave us the tour said that you can't really see how wonderful the Barrier is … not from the river anyway.
They have this little model and he showed us how the Barrier works because in the model you can see the bits under the water that you can't see when you're standing outside looking at the Thames.
He told us what's so important about the Barrier, and how it was getting more and more important. At the end, we all went into a small cinema where they showed us a really old film about how they built the Barrier. That was amazing … they had to stop parts of the river to do it! How can you stop the biggest river in England? When we got outside again, I had changed my way of looking at the Barrier: To me, it really is one of the wonders of the world.
Don't wait till you have friends or visitors staying with you, go there in the holidays (when they have special activities)! You'll like it! It's open seven days a week, and it's only £ 2.00 for adults and £ 1.00 for children.

"**Dad:** What's the formula for water?
Son: H I J K L M N O.
Dad: What?
Son: Our teacher said it was H to O."

How the Thames Barrier works

The Thames Barrier is a series of ten movable gates[1] across the river. When you close the Barrier you close off part of the upper Thames from the sea. When not in use, the six gates cannot be seen because they are lying on the riverbed so the water and ships can get through. When there are dangerous high tides[2], the gates are moved up from the riverbed. Then they form a continuous steel[3] wall – 520 meters from bank to bank. This stops the sea water going up the river to London. The gates are over 20 meters high and each weighs about 3,700 tonnes.
A bad flood[4] in London could be very dangerous for the central part of the City: The London Underground would be flooded, with severe problems for power, gas, telephone and data services.

For hundreds of years, Londoners have built higher and higher walls to keep out the water. But this time, people felt that they – and the millions of tourists travelling to London each year – still wanted to see the river without climbing over high walls. Also, sea levels were getting higher more and more quickly (about 60 cm every century). In 1972, the plans for the Thames Barrier got under way. Nowadays, the Barrier has to be closed more times every year.

[1]**movable gates** [ˌmuːvəbl ˈgeɪts] bewegliche (Schleusen-)Tore • [2]**high tide** [haɪ taɪd] Flut • [3]**steel** [stiːl] Stahl • [3]**flood** [flʌd] Überschwemmung

Great books for the summer

Yes, some people still like a good book, and summer is the best time to sit down on a bench in Greenwich Park, look at the city, get out your favourite book and enjoy the sun … Here are some tips from our team.

Philip Pullman: *The Ruby in the Smoke*
Pullman is a wonderful storyteller – I love his books. Here, he tells the story of Sally Lockhart: She's 16 and lived in London over 100 years ago. When she tries to find out about how her father dies, she kills a man – with just three words: 'The Seven Blessings'. Of course, Sally wants to find out about all the strange letters and about a jewel covered in blood. A good read if you like mysteries – and make sure you watch the film, too. *Tara*

Charlie Higson: *The Young Bond Series* (4 books so far)
Of course you all know James Bond, 007, the most famous spy in the British Secret Services. The writer Ian Fleming wrote about him over 50 years ago, and now his family wanted a modern author to write stories of James's childhood years. How did James become the brilliant agent we know from films? What about his family, his friends, his education? Full of fun, mystery and murder. Very clever! *Sam*

R. L. Stevenson: *Treasure Island*
Even if you can't go away this summer: Why not dream about islands, about treasures and pirates? A classic tale full of great characters. *Terry*

Stephenie Meyer: *The Twilight Saga*
A romantic love affair between a human and a vampire. Maybe you're all a bit young for this, but it's a great read, and it will have you crying – and biting – all four of the books. *Daisy*

Historic Britain – The Romans

Our class project this year (in Year 8) was about the Romans in Britain. At first some of us thought this was really boring … but then we decided to take a look at the Romans in Bath, and suddenly things got interesting. Here are some of our results:

- The Romans came to Britain in 42 AD. They stayed for about 400 years.
- They built roads, walls and toilets!
- They loved baths and tried to find hot springs[1] wherever they went.
- In the first century, they started building baths around the hot springs at Bath. The Celts already knew about the hot water in 860 BC – that's 2,870 years ago!
- The Romans built temples and halls and Bath became the most famous public bath in Britain.
- The Roman name for Bath was Aquae Sulis – the Waters of Sulis.
- There were hot and cold rooms.
- Many rooms had mosaic floors.
- The water still flows from the spring into the corner of the Great Bath at a constant temperature of 46°C, and it still flows out into the River Avon through the Roman drain[2]!
- In the Middle Ages, people forgot about the Roman baths, which fell into ruin. Houses were built on top.
- In the 18th century, Bath became fashionable[3] again, with baths built around some of the other springs.
- Today you can go and see the Roman baths in Bath. You can swim in the water from a hot spring, too, in one of the modern spa baths.

[1]**hot spring** [ˌhɒt ˈsprɪŋ] heiße Quelle • [2]**drain** [dreɪn] Abwasserkanal • [3]**fashionable** [ˈfæʃənəbl] modisch

QUIZ PAGE

PICTURE PUZZLE

a) Does the picture show
   1. a bird?
   2. an underwater animal?
   3. a musical instrument?

b) Where in Britain can you find it?

(The answers are on p. 32.)

TRACKWORD

How many words with three letters or more can you find?
You can go up ↑, down ↓, left ←, right → or diagonally ↖ ↗ ↙ ↘.

You can make the third person singular of a verb with an *s*, but not plurals.

I	C	D	A	H
D	E	A	S	Y
N	X	H	T	I
U	T	O	E	N
B	O	S	W	G

WORDSEARCH

Find the words from this issue of TOG.
They go up ↑, down ↓, left ←, right → and diagonally ↘ ↙.

barrier famous homeless language marathon millennium monster national natural spring walk

M	O	K	S	Q	N	W	A	L	K	F	L	L	J
J	I	D	S	U	A	R	L	L	S	A	V	M	R
A	F	L	E	B	T	U	Y	P	L	M	C	X	M
R	Y	A	L	N	I	T	R	E	A	O	J	O	S
E	C	N	E	E	O	I	G	O	R	U	N	Z	H
I	L	G	M	R	N	O	X	V	U	S	W	Y	K
R	G	U	O	G	A	N	O	H	T	A	R	A	M
R	N	A	H	R	L	Z	I	E	A	J	N	L	D
A	W	G	Q	O	G	E	R	U	N	N	U	K	R
B	X	E	B	V	C	Z	O	W	M	A	V	B	O

Autumn term, page 11

Sudoku

1	5	2	3	7	8	6	4	9
9	3	4	6	2	5	8	7	1
7	8	6	9	4	1	5	3	2
6	1	7	2	5	3	9	8	4
5	4	3	8	9	6	2	1	7
8	2	9	4	1	7	3	6	5
2	6	1	5	8	4	7	9	3
4	9	8	7	3	2	1	5	6
3	7	5	1	6	9	4	2	8

Find the words

F	O	X							
F	I	S	H						
F	O	U	N	D					
F	L	U	F	F	Y				
F	L	A	V	O	U	R			
F	R	I	E	N	D	L	Y		
F	L	A	M	I	N	G	O	S	
F	I	G	U	R	E	H	E	A	D

Spring term, page 21

Places in Greenwich: The first name is Thomas Tallis School and the second is the name of the famous ship, the *Cutty Sark*. The next name is the Royal Observatory and then comes the name of something you can see there: the Prime Meridian. Down the hill are the Queen's House and the Royal Naval College and at the bottom of the hill is the River Thames. The extra place that tourists like to visit is the Fan Museum.

Definitions: 1E, 2H, 3A , 4B, 5F, 6D, 7C, 8G

A word snake: momentsaladatextrartistwain

Summer term, page 31

Picture puzzle: It's a picture of bagpipes, (c) a musical instrument that you find in Scotland.

Trackword: ash, axe, boost, boot, cat, dead, dice, die, east, easy, eat, end, get, gets, had, has, hash, haste, hat, head, host, hot, ice, iced, idea, its, net, new, nut, sad, say, sin, sing, sit, south, ten, the, then, tie, tin, toe, went, west

Wordsearch

M	O	K	S	Q	N	W	A	L	K	F	L	L	J
J	I	D	S	U	A	R	L	L	S	A	V	M	R
A	F	L	E	B	T	U	Y	P	L	M	C	X	M
R	Y	A	L	N	I	T	R	E	A	O	J	O	S
E	C	N	E	E	O	I	G	O	R	U	N	Z	H
I	L	G	M	R	N	O	X	V	U	S	W	Y	K
R	G	U	O	G	A	N	O	H	T	A	R	A	M
R	N	A	H	R	L	Z	I	E	A	J	N	L	D
A	W	G	Q	O	G	E	R	U	N	N	U	K	R
B	X	E	B	V	C	Z	O	W	M	A	V	B	O